Once upon a time there was a selfish dog.

One night he was looking for

somewhere to sleep.

He went into a stable.

He saw a cow and a donkey munching

some soft, fresh hay.

'That looks a good place to sleep,'

said the dog.

'Can I sleep in the hay?'
said the dog.

'Yes, you can,' said the cow.
'Yes, you can,' said the donkey.

The dog went to sleep.

The cow went to sleep.
The donkey went to sleep.

'Can I eat the hay now?'
said the cow.

'No,' said the dog.
'I want to sleep here.'

'Can I eat the hay now?'
said the donkey.

'No,' said the dog.
'I want to sleep here.'

'But we want to eat the hay,'
said the cow and the donkey.

'But I want to sleep in the hay,' said the dog.

'Shoo!' said the cow.
'Shoo!' said the donkey.
'We want you to go.'